Fresh & Tasty

Fun food
for children

R&R PUBLICATIONS MARKETING PTY LTD

Published by:
R&R Publications Marketing Pty. Ltd
ACN 083 612 579
PO Box 254, Carlton North, Victoria 3054 Australia
Phone (61 3) 9381 2199 Fax (61 3) 9381 2689
E-mail: info@randrpublications.com.au
Website: www.randrpublications.com.au
Australia wide toll-free: 1800 063 296

©Richard Carroll

Fresh & Tasty Fun food for children

Publisher: Richard Carroll
Cover Designer: Lucy Adams
Typesetter: Elain Wei Voon Loh
Production Manager: Anthony Carroll
Food Photography: Peter Cassidy, Simon Harsett
Home Economist: Bridget Sargeson
Food Stylists: Janet Lodge, Wendy Berecry, Roisin Nield
Recipe Development: Juliet Sykes, Terry Farris,
Anne Sheasby, Penny Farrell, Ellen Argyriou
Proofreader: Cindy Brown

Disclaimer: The nutritional information listed with each recipe does not include the nutrient content of garnishes or any accompaniments not listed in specific quantities in the ingredient list. The nutritional information for each recipe is an estimate only, and may vary depending on the brand of ingredients used, and due to natural biological variations in the composition of natural foods such as meat, fish, fruit and vegetables. The nutritional information was calculated by using the computer program Foodworks dietary analysis software (version 3.01, Xyris Software Pty Ltd. Queensland Australia), and is based on the Australian food composition tables and food manufacturers' data. Where not specified, ingredients are always analysed as average or medium, not small or large. The analysis shown is for 100g of the recipe specified.

Includes Index
ISBN 978-1-74022-350-8

This edition printed February 2007
Computer Typeset in Futura

Printed in Singapore

Cover: Hero Sandwiches, page 19

56

Contents

49

75

Introduction

Fun Food for Children is a cookbook with a difference: the recipes were chosen by children for children; children helped to test them and it was the majority view that decided what should be included. The result is a well-balanced selection of recipes for all ages and all occasions. Brains with parsley sauce and tripe and onions got the thumbs down, but the panel approved plenty of salads, wholefood bakes, fruity desserts and vegetarian dishes alongside old favourites like kebabs, pizza, pasta, chicken drumsticks and sweet treats such as rocky road ice-cream and lamingtons.

Breakfasts and lunches came in for careful scrutiny, with the accent on speedily-prepared dishes for schooldays and some special treats for weekends. Suppers are more substantial, but also take into account the pit-stop factor; some dishes can be made in minutes while others can safely be put on hold for latecomers. Teenagers had the strongest opinions. It was they who were particularly concerned about nutrition. This was also the group with the most vegetarians.

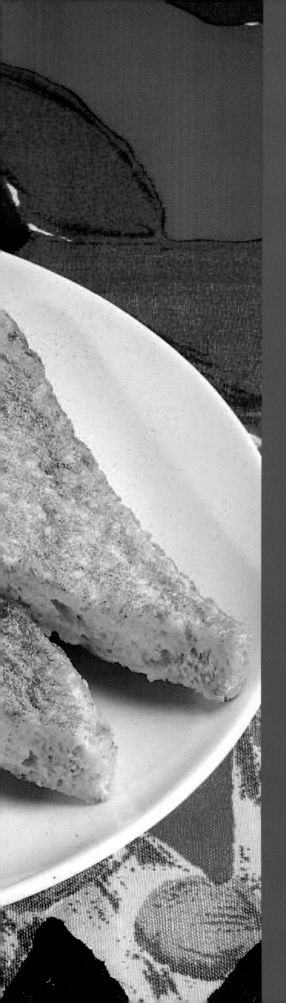

Snacks and Light Meals

Pancake Stacks

125g self-raising flour
2 tbsps sugar
1 egg
170mL milk
30g butter

1. Place flour in sifter or sieve. Sift into large mixing bowl. Add sugar.
2. Break egg into small bowl. Add milk. Whisk.
3. Make a well in centre of flour mixture. Pour in egg mixture. Beat with wooden spoon until smooth.
4. Place a little butter in frying pan. Heat over a medium-high heat until butter melts and sizzles.
5. Pour 3–4 tablespoons of batter into pan. Cook until bubbles form on top of pancake. Turn over. Cook for 1–2 minutes or until second side is brown.
6. Place cooked pancake on plate. Repeat with remaining pancake batter to make 10 pancakes.
7. Stack three or four pancakes on each serving plate. Eat pancakes plain or top with your favourite topping.

Makes 10

Pig Pen

2 tbsps vegetable oil
1 small onion, chopped
1 stick celery, chopped
1 small leek, sliced
200g can chopped tomatoes
1 small carrot, chopped
1 small parsnip, chopped
1 small potato, diced
300mL vegetable stock
black pepper, to taste salt
2 frankfurters, cut into small pieces (optional)
2 slices wholemeal bread

1 Heat 1 tablespoon of the oil in a heavy-based saucepan, then add the onion, celery and leek. Cook, covered, for 5 minutes or until softened, stirring occasionally.

2 Add the tomatoes, carrot, parsnip and potato, then cook for 3–4 minutes longer.

3 Pour the vegetable stock into the pan and season with black pepper and salt. Bring to the boil, cover, then simmer for 30 minutes, or until the vegetables are tender. Remove from the heat and purée the soup with a hand blender until thick but still chunky, or mash with a potato masher. Add the frankfurter pieces, if using, to the purée and heat through for 3 minutes.

4 Meanwhile, use a small pig shaped pastry cutter to stamp out 6 'pigs' from the bread. Heat the remaining oil in a frying pan, then fry the bread pigs for 2–3 minutes on each side until golden. Drain on kitchen towels. Serve the croûtons with the soup.

Serves 2

Note: This chunky soup is delicious and easy to make, but you will need a pig-shaped cutter.

Banana Choc-chip Muffins

1 large ripe banana
1 cup milk
1 egg
60g butter or margarine, melted
170g self-raising flour
120g caster sugar
120g choc bits

1 In a mixing bowl, mash the banana, add the milk, egg and melted butter. Mix well.

2 Stir the flour, sugar and choc bits into the banana mixture, mix only until the ingredients are combined. Spoon mixture into well-greased muffin tins. Bake at 190°C for 20 minutes. Serve warm or cold.

Makes 12

Oven temperature 190°C

Breakfast Smoothie

1 medium ripe banana
340g natural yoghurt
1 egg
honey to taste
nutmeg or cinnamon, to sprinkle

1 Place all ingredients except nutmeg or cinnamon into a blender and blend until fluffy.

2 Pour into glass and sprinkle with nutmeg or cinnamon.

Note: Orange juice can be substituted for the yoghurt for a refreshing change.

Wild Flower Meadow Salad

1 medium egg
60g mixed salad leaves
6 baby corn, thinly sliced into rounds
6 cherry tomatoes, halved
45g seedless white grapes
1 small red eating apple, cored
and diced
60g Gruyère, thinly sliced and
cut into leaf shapes

For the dressing
1 tsp Dijon mustard
2 tbsps olive oil
1 tbsp wine vinegar
2 tbsps natural yoghurt
black pepper, to taste

1 Hard-boil the egg for 10 minutes in a small saucepan of boiling water. Cool under cold running water, peel off the shell, then cut into sixths. Arrange the salad leaves in bowls and scatter over the baby corn, tomatoes, grapes, apple, Gruyère and hard-boiled egg.

2 To make the dressing, mix together the mustard, oil, vinegar, yoghurt and seasoning. Drizzle over the salad.

Serves 2

Note: This colourful selection of grapes, baby corn and cherry tomatoes makes a great imaginary flower meadow. But you can use whatever fruit and vegetables you've got.

Eggs in Ponchos

2 rashers back bacon, cut into small pieces

3 medium eggs

2 tbsps full-fat milk

black pepper, to taste

30g butter

4 tbsps canned chilli beans

2 wheat tortillas

For the guacamole

1 ripe avocado, stoned, peeled and chopped

1 small tomato, chopped, plus 1 tomato, cut into wedges, to garnish

2 spring onions, finely chopped

juice of ¹/₂ lime

¹/₂ tsp chopped fresh coriander (optional)

1   First make the guacamole. Place the avocado, tomato, spring onions, lime juice and coriander, if using, in a bowl. Mash with a fork to combine, then cover and set aside.

2   Place the bacon in a frying pan and fry in its own fat for 3 minutes or until crisp, then set aside. Mix the eggs and milk together with a fork, then season with pepper. Melt the butter in a non-stick saucepan. Add the egg mixture and cook, stirring, for 3 minutes or until the egg is scrambled and well cooked. Gently stir in the bacon pieces.

3   Meanwhile, heat the chilli beans in a saucepan for 4–5 minutes. Place a frying pan over a medium heat, then warm the tortillas, one at a time, for 15 seconds on each side. Transfer to plates, top with the scrambled egg and chilli beans, then wrap each tortilla loosely around its filling. Serve with the guacamole and tomato wedges.

Serves 2

Note: Tortillas are filled with a delicious combination of scrambled egg and chilli beans. Creamy guacamole completes this colourful Mexican-inspired dish.

French Toast

1 egg
60mL milk
1 tsp sugar
½ tsp vanilla essence
2 slices wholemeal bread
cinnamon powder
fruit for serving

1 Place egg, milk, sugar and vanilla into a flat dish, whisk with a fork.
2 Place bread into egg mixture and leave 1–2 minutes.
3 Heat non-stick frying pan, place the bread into the pan and allow to brown before turning to brown other side. Sprinkle with cinnamon and serve with fresh fruit.

Serves 1–2

Hide and Seek

2 medium baking potatoes
butter or sunflower oil for greasing
2 rashers back bacon, cut into small pieces
60g mature cheddar cheese, grated
1 tbsp crème fraîche
2 tsps snipped fresh chives
salt and black pepper, to taste

For the coleslaw
100g red cabbage, shredded
2 spring onions, chopped
1 eating apple, cored and chopped
1 small carrot, grated
2 tbsps mayonnaise

1 Preheat the oven to 220°C. Rub the skins of the potatoes with butter or oil. Put the potatoes in the oven and cook for 1 hour or until soft in the centre.

2 Place the bacon in a frying pan and cook in its own fat for 3 minutes or until crisp, then set aside. To make the coleslaw, combine the cabbage, spring onions, apple, carrot and mayonnaise, and refrigerate until needed.

3 When the potatoes are cooked, slice the top off each one and reserve. Scoop out the centres and place in a bowl with the cheese, crème fraîche, chives and bacon pieces. Mix well with a fork and season with salt and black pepper. Pile the mixture back into the empty potato skins and return to the oven for 5 minutes to heat through. Replace the reserved potato tops over the filled potatoes and serve with the coleslaw.

Serves 2

Note: When children lift the potato lids, they'll discover a delicious, creamy, cheese and bacon filling. Use any leftover potato mixture as a base for making fish cakes.

Oven temperature 220°C

Sheep and Dip

For the 'sheep'
175g shortcrust pastry
milk for brushing
1 small cauliflower, cut into florets

For the dip
15g butter
15g plain flour
150mL full-fat milk
100mL apple juice
125g mature cheddar, grated
salt and black pepper
1 spring onion, finely chopped

1   Preheat the oven to 200°C. Roll out the pastry thinly on a floured surface. Stamp out 8–10 sheep shapes, using a 5cm fluted pastry cutter for the bodies and a 3cm cutter for the heads. Cut out 2½ cm strips for the legs. Brush with milk and stick together, then place on a baking sheet. Bake for 10 minutes or until golden. Transfer to a rack to cool for 20 minutes.

2   Meanwhile, make the dip. Melt the butter in a saucepan over a low heat. Sprinkle in the flour and cook for 1 minute, stirring. Remove the pan from the heat, then gradually add the milk, whisking all the time. Return to the heat and cook gently, stirring, for 3–4 minutes or until thickened. Gradually stir in the juice, then simmer for 2 minutes, stirring. Add the cheese, stir until melted, season with salt and black pepper, then keep warm.

3   Boil the cauliflower for 5 minutes or until tender. Pour the dip into a bowl and sprinkle with spring onion. Serve with the cauliflower and pastry 'sheep'.

Serves 4

Note:These fluffy sheep shapes transform cauliflower cheese into a magical meal for small children. This is sure to be a winning combination at birthday parties.

Oven temperature 200°C

Giant Katherine Wheels

400g shortcrust pastry
plain flour for dusting
100g mature cheddar, grated
2 tbsps freshly grated Parmesan
2 tbsps tomato purée
2 tbsps pesto of choice
1 medium egg, beaten, for glazing
vegetable oil for greasing

1 Preheat the oven to 190°C. Roll out the pastry on a floured surface and cut to make 2 rectangles measuring 20 x 25cm. Mix together the cheddar and Parmesan, then set aside.

2 Spread 1 sheet of pastry with the tomato purée. Place the second sheet of pastry on top, spread with the pesto, then sprinkle with the cheese. Roll up the pastry from the shorter side with the filling inside. Brush the roll with the egg and refrigerate for 20 minutes.

3 Cut the roll into 1cm slices and place on greased baking sheets. Bake for 20 minutes or until golden. Leave to cool slightly on wire racks.

Makes 10

Note: An indoor sparkler fizzing in the middle of these tasty tomato and pesto pastry swirls will cause a sensation! But – as always – take great care with fireworks.

Oven temperature 190°C

Cheesy Potato Frittata

1 cold cooked potato
2 rashers bacon
4 eggs
freshly ground black pepper
30g butter
3 tbsps grated tasty cheese
(mature cheddar)

1 Cut potato into 1cm cubes. Set aside.

2 Cut rind from bacon. Using scissors cut bacon into strips. Set aside.

3 Break eggs into bowl. Add black pepper to taste. Whisk. Set aside.

4 Place butter in frying pan. Heat over a medium heat until butter melts and sizzles. Add bacon. Cook, stirring, for 2–3 minutes or until bacon is cooked.

5 Add potato to pan. Cook, stirring, for 5 minutes or until potato is brown.

6 Pour egg mixture into pan. Turn heat to low. Cook for 10 minutes or until frittata is almost set.

7 Preheat grill to high.

8 Sprinkle top of frittata with cheese. Place pan under grill. Cook for 2–3 minutes or until cheese melts. Cut frittata into wedges to serve.

Serves 4

Hero Sandwiches

1 long French loaf
4 tbsps mayonnaise
1 tbsp wholegrain mustard
2 tbsps natural yoghurt
6 large lettuce leaves
125g thinly sliced ham, roast beef
or turkey
60g thinly sliced salami
2 tomatoes
4 slices tasty cheese (mature cheddar)
string for tying

1 Cut French loaf in half lengthwise. Set aside.
2 Place mayonnaise, mustard and yoghurt in bowl. Mix.
3 Spread over cut sides of loaf. Set aside.
4 Place lettuce leaves on bottom half of loaf. Top with ham, beef or turkey and salami.
5 Slice tomatoes thickly.
6 Place tomatoes and cheese on top of meat. Top with other half of loaf.
7 Tie loaf at intervals with string. Cut into four.

Serves 4

Pretty Posy Pizzas

For the pizzas
125g self-raising flour, sifted
1 tsp dried oregano
2 tbsps olive oil
4 tbsps cold water

For the topping
1 small onion, finely chopped
200g can chopped tomatoes
1 tsp tomato purée
1 tsp chopped fresh basil, plus leaves to garnish
black pepper, to taste
9 small slices pepperoni, halved
2 slices fresh mozzarella

1 Place the onion, tomatoes, tomato purée, basil and pepper to taste in a saucepan. Simmer for 20 minutes, stirring occasionally, or until thickened.

2 Meanwhile, make the pizza bases. Put the flour and oregano into a large bowl, season, then add 1 tablespoon of the oil and 4 tablespoons of cold water. Mix with your hands to make a soft dough.

3 Turn the dough out onto a floured board. Knead for 1 minute, until smooth, then halve it and roll each piece into a 13cm round. Heat the remaining oil in a large, non-stick frying pan and gently cook the bases, one at a time, for 5 minutes on each side or until golden.

4 Preheat the grill to high. Spread the tomato sauce over the bases. Make a flower shape on the top of each pizza using pepperoni slices for petals and a slice of mozzarella for the centre. Place under the grill for 2 minutes to melt the cheese. Garnish with basil.

Serves 2

Note: These homemade pizzas are pretty and delicious, and really quick to make. Children can decorate their own pizzas with a variety of their favourite toppings.

Pick-up Sticks

6 wooden skewers
¼ red capsicum and
¼ yellow capsicum, cut into small chunks
4 button mushrooms, quartered
1 small zucchini, thickly sliced and halved lengthways
100g tofu (beancurd), cubed

For the marinade
1 tbsp lemon juice
1 tsp clear honey
2 tbsps light soy sauce
black pepper, to taste

For the dipping sauce
1 tsp olive oil
1 small clove garlic, chopped
3 tbsps plum sauce
1 tsp soft light brown sugar
100mL vegetable stock

1 Soak 6 wooden skewers in water for 10 minutes to prevent them burning under the grill. To make the marinade, mix together the lemon juice, honey, soy sauce and black pepper in a large, non-metallic dish. Add the red and yellow capsicum, mushrooms, zucchini and tofu (beancurd) and stir to coat. Place in the fridge for 1 hour to marinate.

2 Preheat the grill to medium. Thread the vegetables and tofu (beancurd) onto the skewers. Grill for 6 minutes, turning skewers occasionally, until evenly cooked.

3 Meanwhile, make the dipping sauce. Heat the oil in a saucepan. Add the garlic and cook, stirring, for 1 minute or until softened. Stir in the plum sauce, sugar and stock and boil rapidly for 5 minutes or until the sauce has reduced and thickened slightly. Allow to cool for a few minutes, then serve with the kebabs.

Makes 6

Note: For a main meal, serve these vegetable kebabs on a bed of salad leaves with rice or noodles and dress with the fruity dipping sauce. Blunt the skewers for extra safety.

Savoury Potatoes

Base Potatoes
8 potatoes, scrubbed

1 Boil, steam or microwave potatoes until tender.

2 Cut a cross in the top of each potato and press to open out. Divide topping of your choice (see below) between potatoes and place under a preheated hot grill for 4–5 minutes, if necessary, to warm filling.

Cheese and Chive Topping
185g reduced-fat ricotta cheese
4 tbsps grated reduced-fat cheddar cheese
2 tbsps snipped fresh chives
freshly ground black pepper

1 Place ricotta and cheddar cheeses, chives, and black pepper to taste in a bowl and mix to combine.

Mushroom Topped Potatoes
2 tsps polyunsaturated margarine
1 small onion, chopped
250g button mushrooms, sliced
1 large tomato, chopped
1 tbsp chopped fresh basil
freshly ground black pepper

1 Melt margarine in a small saucepan and cook onion for 3–4 minutes or until soft. Add mushrooms and tomatoes and cook for 4–5 minutes longer. Stir basil through and season to taste with black pepper.

Cheesy Bean Potatoes
250mL skim milk
2 tbsps cornflour
375g canned soya beans, drained
60g grated reduced-fat cheddar cheese
2 tbsps grated Parmesan cheese
¼ tsp grated nutmeg
1 tbsp chopped fresh parsley
freshly ground black pepper

1 Gently heat 185mL milk in a saucepan, without boiling, for 3–4 minutes. Combine cornflour with remaining milk and stir into pan. Cook, stirring constantly, until sauce thickens. Stir in soya beans, cheddar and parmesan cheeses and nutmeg and cook for 2–3 minutes or until heated through. Stir in parsley and black pepper to taste.

Each Serves 4

Meat Main Meals

Tasty Tacos Photographed above

1 large onion
2 cloves garlic (if desired)
1 tbsp vegetable oil
500g lean beef mince
30g packet taco seasoning mix
125mL water
3 tbsps tomato sauce
8 taco shells
4 large lettuce leaves
2 tomatoes
4 tbsps grated tasty cheese (mature cheddar)

1 Preheat oven to 180°C.
2 Peel onion. Chop. Set aside.
3 Crush garlic. Set aside.
4 Place oil in frying pan. Heat over a medium heat until hot. Add onion and garlic. Cook, stirring, for 5–6 minutes.
5 Add beef. Cook, stirring, for 5 minutes.
6 Stir in taco seasoning mix, water and tomato sauce. Cook, stirring for 5 minutes.
7 Place taco shells on baking tray. Heat in oven for 5 minutes.
8 Roll lettuce leaves. Cut into strips. Set aside.
9 Cut tomatoes into small pieces. Set aside.
10 Spoon beef mixture into taco shells. Top with lettuce, tomato and cheese.

Serves 4

Oven temperature 180°C

Ham and Potato Omelette

1 tsp vegetable oil, butter or margarine
1 small slice ham, chopped
1 small potato, finely chopped
1–2 tbsps frozen peas or sweetcorn kernels, rinsed
1 egg, lightly beaten
2 tbsps milk

1 Heat oil, butter or margarine in a small frying pan over a medium heat, add ham, potato and peas or sweetcorn and cook, stirring frequently, for 5–10 minutes or until potato is tender.
2 Place egg and milk in a bowl and whisk to combine. Pour egg mixture over potato mixture in pan, reduce heat and cook, without stirring, for 3–4 minutes or until omelette is just firm.

Makes 1

Crunchy Cutlets

1 tbsp vegetable oil
6 lamb cutlets, trimmed and slightly flattened

Crunchy coating
1 egg, lightly beaten
45g breadcrumbs, made from stale bread
30g cornflakes, crushed

1   Place egg in a shallow dish. Place breadcrumbs and crushed cornflakes in a separate dish and mix to combine. Dip cutlets in egg, then in breadcrumb mixture to coat.

2   Heat oil in a frying pan over a medium heat until hot, add cutlets and cook for 2 minutes on each side or until cooked through and golden.

Serves 3–6

Plough the Fields and Scatter

125g potatoes, diced
1 tbsp full-fat milk
30g butter
2 tsps sunflower oil
1 onion, chopped
1 small clove garlic, crushed
1 carrot, diced
250g minced lamb
2 tsps mixed fresh herbs, such as thyme and rosemary
black pepper, to taste
150mL lamb stock
dash of Worcestershire sauce
2 tbsps fresh breadcrumbs
30g mature cheddar, grated
40g frozen peas
2 tsps snipped fresh chives

1   Cook the potatoes in boiling water for 15 minutes or until tender, then drain. Mash with the milk and half the butter. Meanwhile, heat the oil in a heavy-based frying pan, add the onion and garlic and cook for 5 minutes or until softened. Add the carrot and cook for another 3 minutes to soften slightly.

2   Add the minced lamb and herbs to the onion and garlic and break up the mince with a wooden spoon. Cook for 10 minutes or until the mince has browned. Season, then add the stock and simmer, uncovered, for 20 minutes or until most of the liquid has evaporated. Add the Worcestershire sauce.

3   Preheat the grill to high. Mix together the lamb mixture and potatoes, then place in a flameproof dish. Sprinkle with the breadcrumbs and cheese. Drag the handle of a wooden spoon along the top to make furrows, then grill for 3–4 minutes, until golden. Meanwhile, fry the peas in the remaining butter for 1–2 minutes. Scatter over the 'field' with the chives.

Serves 2

Note: This meal-in-a-dish can be served on its own, but if you get carried away you can complete the rural scene by adding a hedgerow made from steamed broccoli florets.

Pot Plants

1 red and 1 yellow capsicum
1 tbsp balsamic vinegar
2 tbsps olive oil
2 baby corns
1 small onion, chopped
1 small clove garlic, chopped
75g minced lamb
1 tsp tomato purée
30g bulgar wheat
150mL lamb stock
30g frozen peas
30g ready-to-eat dried apricots, chopped
1 tsp ground coriander
salt and black pepper, to taste
watercress sprigs to garnish

1 Preheat the oven to 200°C. Slice off and discard the tops of the peppers and deseed. Square off the bottoms and stand on a baking sheet. Sprinkle with the balsamic vinegar and 1 tablespoon of the oil. Cook for 15 minutes, then add the baby corns to the sheet. Cook for 5–10 minutes, until everything is tender.

2 Meanwhile, heat the remaining oil in a large saucepan, add the onion and garlic and fry for 5 minutes or until softened. Add the minced lamb and cook for 5 minutes or until browned. Stir in the tomato purée, bulgar wheat, stock, peas, apricots and coriander, then season with salt and black pepper. Bring to the boil, then simmer for 15 minutes or until the stock has been absorbed, stirring occasionally.

3 Place the capsicum on plates and fill with the lamb mixture. Insert a baby corn and watercress sprigs into the top of each one for the pot plants.

Serves 2

Note: This is a great way to get children to eat fresh vegetables. But if they don't like capsicum, you can always use two hollowed-out large beefsteak tomatoes instead.

Oven temperature 200°C

Noodle Caboodle Photographed opposite

125g dried egg noodles
2 tsps vegetable oil
2 spring onions, chopped
1 small clove garlic, crushed
75g cucumber, cut into thin sticks
2 baby corn, sliced
4 cherry tomatoes
50g smoked ham, cut into cubes
1 tbsp light soy sauce
black pepper, to taste

1 Prepare the noodles according to the packet instructions, then drain well.

2 Heat the oil in a wok or large, heavy-based frying pan over a high heat. Add the spring onions, garlic, cucumber, corn, tomatoes and ham and stir-fry for 3 minutes or until the vegetables are tender and the tomatoes are beginning to split. Stir in the soy sauce and season.

3 Add the noodles to the vegetable mixture, toss well and stir-fry for 1–2 minutes, until heated through.

Serves 2

Note: If you're feeling brave, you can add to the fun of this healthy Chinese stir-fry by letting children eat it with chopsticks! But keep the kitchen towels handy!

Sticks and Stones

For the 'sticks'
2 tsps vegetable oil
1 small red onion, thinly sliced
1 tsp soft dark brown sugar

For the 'stones'
125g lean minced pork
60g rindless back bacon, finely chopped
1 tbsp vegetable oil

For the tomato sauce
230g can chopped tomatoes
pinch of dried oregano
1 tsp sun-dried tomato purée
black pepper, to taste

1 First make the sauce. Put the tomatoes, oregano, tomato purée and pepper into a saucepan. Cook gently for 20 minutes or until the sauce thickens, stirring occasionally.

2 Meanwhile, make the sticky caramelised onions. Heat the oil in a heavy-based frying pan, add the onion and cook gently for 10 minutes or until softened, stirring occasionally. Add the sugar and cook gently for 2–3 minutes, stirring, until brown and sticky. Remove from the pan and set aside.

3 Make the 'stones'. Mix the pork and bacon in a bowl and roll into 8 walnut-sized balls, using your hands. Heat the oil in a frying pan and cook the meatballs for 15 minutes, turning occasionally, until cooked and browned. Pour the tomato sauce over and simmer for 5 minutes, then transfer to bowls. Top each serving with a spoonful of onions.

Serves 2

Note: Sticky caramelised onions and meatball 'stones' won't break any bones and will make supper time fun. Serve them with rice to soak up the thick tomato sauce.

Jack and the Bean Pork

250g potatoes, diced
1 small carrot, diced
knob of butter
black pepper, to taste
1 tsp vegetable oil
3 spring onions, chopped
1 small clove garlic, crushed
8 cocktail sausages or 4 pork sausages, halved widthways
200g canned ratatouille
125g canned mixed beans, rinsed and drained
25g cheddar, grated
thin strips of zucchini
whole snow peas

1   Cook the potatoes and carrot in boiling water for 10–15 minutes, until tender, then drain well and mash with the butter and pepper.

2   Heat the oil in a saucepan. Fry the spring onions and garlic for 3 minutes or until softened. Add the sausages and cook for 10–15 minutes, until browned and cooked through. Stir in the ratatouille and beans and heat through, then season again.

3   Preheat the grill to medium. Transfer the sausage mixture to a flameproof dish, top with the mash and sprinkle with cheese. Grill for 3 minutes or until the cheese browns. Meanwhile, cook the zucchini strips and snowpeas in boiling water for 2 minutes to soften. Arrange the zucchini strips on top of the pie in the shape of a beanstalk, using the snow peas as leaves.

Serves 2

Note: This comforting dish of mixed beans and vegetables will transport children to the fairytale world of giants and Daisy the cow. Perhaps the beans are magic!

Basic Meatloaf

1 beef stock cube
60mL hot water
1 onion
1 carrot
2 eggs
1 tsp mixed dried herbs
1 tsp Worcestershire sauce
4 slices stale wholemeal bread
500g lean beef mince
freshly ground black pepper
vegetable oil

1 Preheat oven to 180°C.

2 Place stock cube and water in large bowl. Mix. Cool.

3 Peel onion. Grate. Set aside.

4 Peel carrot. Grate. Set aside.

5 Add eggs, herbs and Worcestershire sauce to bowl. Whisk.

6 Place bread slices in food processor or blender. Process to make breadcrumbs.

7 Add breadcrumbs and beef mince to bowl. Add black pepper to taste. Mix.

8 Brush loaf tin lightly with vegetable oil. Spoon mince mixture into tin. Bake for 40–45 minutes or until cooked. Drain carefully. Stand for 10 minutes. Turn out. Cut into slices.

Serves 4

Making breadcrumbs: If you do not have a food processor or blender make breadcrumbs by rubbing the bread against a grater.

Oven temperature 180°C

Honey Beef

2 tsps oil

500g lean rump steak, cut into thin strips

1 parsnip, cut into thin strips

1 red capsicum, cut into thin strips

4 spinach leaves, shredded

3 spring onions, cut diagonally into 2½ cm lengths

1 clove garlic, crushed

2 tsps grated fresh ginger

90mL reduced-salt soy sauce

2 tsps cornflour blended with 2 tbsps dry sherry

2 tsps honey

1 Heat 2 teaspoons oil in a frying pan or wok over a medium heat, add beef, parsnip, red capsicum, spinach and spring onions and stir-fry for 2–3 minutes or until meat changes colour. Remove mixture from pan and set aside.

2 Add remaining oil to pan and heat. Add garlic and ginger and stir-fry for 1–2 minutes, then return beef mixture to the pan. Combine soy sauce, cornflour mixture and honey, stir into pan and cook, stirring, for 1–2 minutes or until heated through. Serve immediately.

Serves 4

34

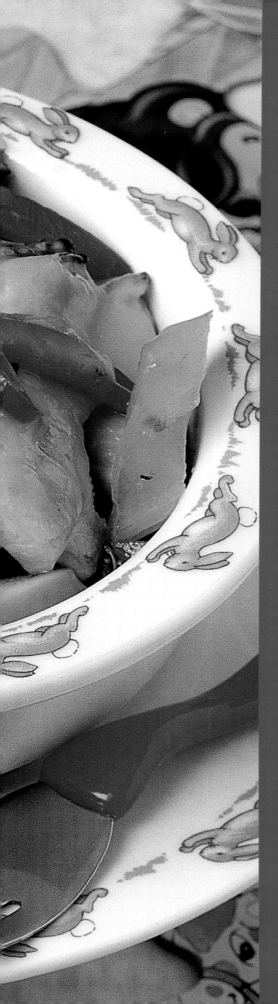

Poultry
main meals

Mango Chicken Stir-Fry

1 tsp vegetable oil
¼ boneless chicken breast fillet, cut into slivers
¼ red capsicum, thinly sliced
60g sliced broccoli or snow peas
⅓ stalk celery, sliced
90mL mango or apricot purée
½ tsp cornflour blended with 2 tsps water

1. Heat oil in a frying pan over a medium heat, add chicken and stir-fry for 3 minutes or until golden.
2. Add red capsicum, broccoli or snow peas, celery and mango or apricot purée and simmer, stirring frequently, for 8 minutes or until chicken and vegetables are tender.
3. Stir cornflour mixture into pan and cook, stirring, for 1 minute longer or until mixture thickens. Cool slightly and serve.

Serves 1

Squirrel Feasts

2 tsps parsley and thyme stuffing mix
60g pork sausage meat
2 skinless boneless chicken thighs
olive oil for brushing
cocktil sticks
¼ tsp dried thyme
2 carrots to garnish
peas to serve

1   Preheat the oven to 190°C. Combine the stuffing mix with 1 tablespoon of boiling water, set aside for 3 minutes, then mix in the sausage meat. Open out the chicken thighs and divide the stuffing mixture between them. Roll them up, brush with oil, then secure with cocktail sticks. Sprinkle over the thyme. Place in an ovenproof dish, seam-side down, and roast for 35 minutes or until cooked through and golden.

2   Meanwhile, make the squirrel tails. Cut 2 thin lengthways slices from 1 carrot for the tails. Cut diagonal slits down both sides of each slice, then place in ice-cold water for 15 minutes or until slightly curled. Carve 2 squirrel heads from the remaining carrot. Remove the cocktail sticks from the chicken, place on a plate, lean the carrot tails behind and balance the carrot heads on top. Spoon peas around.

Serves 2

Note: Make these squirrels as a special treat – they're filled with a delicious herby sausage stuffing. If you're giving them to young children, don't forget to remove the cocktail sticks.

Oven temperature 190°C

Farm Barn

250g fresh breaded chicken pieces
250g pack frozen potato waffles
4 frozen crispy vegetable fingers
4 small tomatoes
olive oil for roasting
250g frozen mixed vegetables
4 tbsps baked beans

1. Preheat the oven to 220°C. Put the chicken pieces, waffles and vegetable fingers on baking trays and cook for 15 minutes, turning once, until cooked through and golden.

2. Meanwhile, slice the tops off the tomatoes, scoop out the seeds and discard. Sprinkle with oil. Place on a baking tray and cook for 3 minutes or until softened. Cook the vegetables in boiling water for 3–5 minutes, until tender, then drain and keep warm. Heat the beans in a saucepan.

3. Fill the tomatoes with the beans. To assemble the barn, arrange 3 tomatoes on a large plate and stand the waffles upright around them to make 4 walls. Place the vegetable fingers over the waffles for rafters, then arrange the chicken pieces on top to make a roof. Spoon mixed vegetables around the outside of the 'barn' to hold up the walls and put 1 tomato outside as a plant pot.

Serves 2

Note: Get the children to guess what's inside the barn before they tuck in. You can put mushrooms or anything else you like inside – you don't have to use tomatoes.

Oven temperature 220°C

Chicken Satays

2 boneless chicken breast fillets
bamboo skewers
90g peanut butter
125mL water
60mL coconut milk
1 tbsp reduced-salt soy sauce
2 tbsps vegetable oil

1 Cut chicken lengthwise into strips. Thread chicken onto bamboo skewers and cut off sharp ends.

2 Place peanut butter, water, coconut milk and soy sauce in a bowl and mix to combine. Brush mixture over chicken to coat.

3 Heat oil in a frying pan over a medium heat, add satays and cook for 2 minutes each side or until chicken is cooked and tender.

Serves 4

Chicken Nuggets

500g chicken mince
1 egg, lightly beaten
45g breadcrumbs, made from stale bread
60g cottage cheese, mashed
2 tbsps finely chopped fresh parsley (optional)
125g dried breadcrumbs
vegetable oil for shallow-frying

1 Place chicken mince, egg, soft breadcrumbs, cottage cheese and parsley (if using) in a bowl and mix well to combine.

2 Take 2 tablespoons of mixture, shape into balls, then flatten slightly and gently press into dried breadcrumbs to coat. Repeat to use all remaining mixture.

3 Heat 1 cm oil in a frying pan over a medium heat until hot, add nuggets and cook for 2 minutes each side or until cooked through and golden. Drain on absorbent kitchen paper, cool slightly and serve.

Makes 24

Oven-fried Chicken

150mL natural low fat yoghurt
1 tsp lemon juice
2 tbsps apricot or peach chutney
125g packet dried breadcrumbs
6 chicken drumsticks
parsley sprigs for garnish

1 Preheat oven to 180°C Purée the yoghurt, lemon juice and chutney in a blender or food processor; transfer to a shallow bowl. Spread out the breadcrumbs in a similar bowl.

2 Coat each drumstick in yoghurt mixture, then roll in bread-crumbs. Arrange on a baking sheet and bake for 45 minutes or until cooked through. Garnish and serve.

Makes 6

Oven temperature 180°C

Rookery Cookery

sunflower oil for greasing and frying

150g skinless boneless chicken breast, minced

2 tbsps fresh breadcrumbs

1 tbsp chopped fresh parsley

1 tsp dried thyme

1 tsp brown sauce

2 medium eggs, beaten

black pepper, to taste

250g waxy potatoes, peeled and grated

1 small onion, finely chopped

For the sauce

1 tbsp crème fraîche

1/2 tsp mild mustard

2 tsps snipped fresh chives

1 To make the sauce, combine the crème fraîche, mustard and chives, then cover and refrigerate.

2 Preheat the grill to high. Cover the grill pan rack with foil and lightly grease. Mix together the chicken, breadcrumbs, parsley, thyme, brown sauce and half the beaten egg, then season with black pepper. Shape into 8 'eggs', using your hands. Grill for 5–10 minutes, turning occasionally, until browned.

3 Meanwhile, make the nests. Place the grated potato in a tea towel and squeeze out any excess water. Put into a bowl with the onion, stir in the rest of the beaten egg and season. Divide the mixture in half, shape into rounds and press to flatten slightly. Heat a little oil in a large, heavy-based frying pan. Cook the rounds for 5–6 minutes on each side, until golden.

4 Make a hollow in the centre of each nest, drain them on kitchen towels, then place on plates. Spoon over the sauce, then top each with 4 'eggs'.

Serves 2

Note: Hatch a tea-time surprise for children with these golden, crunchy potato nests, topped with a creamy sauce and filled with four delicious bird's eggs.

Fish Main Meals

Crunchy Fish Sticks

3 potatoes, chopped
375g canned tuna in brine, drained and flaked
1 egg, lightly beaten
125g breadcrumbs, made from stale bread
vegetable oil for shallow-frying

1 Boil, steam or microwave potatoes until tender. Place in a bowl and mash until smooth. Add tuna and egg to potatoes and mix well to combine.

2 Take 2 tablespoons of mixture, shape into thick fingers or sticks and press into breadcrumbs to coat. Repeat to use all remaining mixture.

3 Heat 1 cm oil in a frying pan over a medium heat until hot, add fish sticks and cook for 3–4 minutes each side or until cooked through and golden. Drain on absorbent kitchen paper, cool slightly and serve.

Makes 24

Cheesy Salmon Patties

315g drained canned butterbeans

200g can red salmon, drained, bones and skin removed

125g mashed potato

90g cheddar cheese, grated

30g grated Parmesan cheese

1 small onion, finely chopped

1 tbsp finely snipped chives

60g plain flour

2 tbsps lemon juice

1 egg, lightly beaten

60g dried breadcrumbs

oil for deep frying

1   Mash butterbeans and salmon to a paste. Add potato, cheeses, onion, chives, flour and lemon juice. Mix well, then add enough egg to bind.

2   Divide mixture evenly into 6–8 portions and form each into a patty. Toss each patty in breadcrumbs until evenly covered.

3   Heat the oil in a large frying pan. Add the patties, pressing them down with a fish slice to flatten. Cook for 2 minutes on each side until golden.

Makes 6–8

Pansies

60g sweet potato, diced

1 tsp sunflower oil, plus extra for brushing and deep-frying

2 spring onions, finely chopped

100g can tuna in spring water, drained

1 tbsp sweetcorn, drained

½ small red capsicum, finely chopped

dash of Worcestershire sauce

1 tbsp plain flour

1 tbsp full-fat milk

black pepper, to taste

1 small raw beetroot or 1 large carrot, thinly sliced

1 Cook the sweet potato in boiling water for 10 minutes or until tender. Drain well, then mash. Heat the oil in a frying pan, add the spring onions and fry for 3 minutes or until softened.

2 Preheat the grill to medium. Place the sweet potato, spring onions, tuna, sweetcorn, red capsicum, Worcestershire sauce and flour in a bowl and mix in the milk.

Season with black pepper, then shape into 4 round cakes with your hands. Brush the tops with oil and grill for 5 minutes. Turn over, brush with oil again and grill for a further 5 minutes or until golden. Drain on kitchen towels and keep warm.

3 Meanwhile, heat 2½ cm of oil in a large saucepan. Fry the beetroot or carrot slices for 3–5 minutes, until crisp. Drain on kitchen towels. To serve, place 2 fish cakes on each plate and top each cake with 4–5 beetroot or carrot slices to make the pansy petals.

Serves 2

Note: Brightly coloured beetroot or carrot 'pansies' make a delicious topping for these tasty tuna fish cakes. Serve them with some baby carrots and courgettes.

Little Fishes

100g long-grain rice
1 medium egg
200g smoked haddock
200ml full-fat milk
25g cooked peeled prawns, defrosted
if frozen
1 tsp lemon juice
pinch of nutmeg
pinch of curry powder
1–2 tbsps chopped fresh parsley
3 tbsps single cream
black pepper, to taste
15g butter, plus extra for greasing
2 slices of bread
1/2 lemon, cut into quarters

1 Preheat the oven to 180°C. Cook the rice according to the packet instructions, then drain. Meanwhile, hard-boil the egg for 10 minutes. Shell under cold water and finely chop. Put the haddock into a saucepan, cover with the milk and poach for 6–8 minutes, until just firm. Drain well, then flake the flesh, removing any bones and skin.

2 Place the egg, fish, rice and prawns in a bowl. Stir in the lemon juice, nutmeg, curry powder, parsley, cream and black pepper. Transfer to a greased ovenproof dish. Dot the butter over the top, cover and cook for 25 minutes.

3 Meanwhile, toast the bread, then cut out fish shapes. Serve the rice dish with lemon wedges and the fish-shaped toasts.

Serves 2

Note: This fishy dishy is made from haddock, prawns and rice. The fish toasts are a great touch and will net you plenty of praise. They're easy to do with a small sharp knife.

Oven temperature 180°C

Starfish and Sea Chest

100g potato, diced
100g skinless cod fillets
150mL full-fat milk
1 tbsp finely chopped parsley
black pepper, to taste
1 small egg, beaten
2 tbsps fresh breadcrumbs
3 tbsps sunflower oil
2 medium waxy potatoes, cut into 1cm thick chips
125g green cabbage, finely shredded

1 Boil the potato for 10 minutes or until tender, then drain and mash. Place the cod in a saucepan and cover with the milk. Poach for 5 minutes or until firm, then drain and flake, removing any bones.

2 Mix together the mash, cod and parsley and black pepper. Divide the mixture into 2 and mould each half into a star shape, using your hands or a 7½ cm star-shaped cutter. Dip the starfish into the egg, then the breadcrumbs. Heat 1 tablespoon of the oil in a large, non-stick frying pan and cook the starfish for 5–7 minutes, turning once, until cooked and golden. Drain on kitchen towels and keep warm.

3 Heat the remaining oil in the frying pan, until hot but not smoking. Drain, then dry the chips in a clean tea towel. Fry for 7–10 minutes, until cooked and golden, then drain on kitchen towels.

4 Meanwhile, steam the cabbage for 4–5 minutes until tender. To serve, build a square of chips to make a sea chest, then arrange the 'seaweed' cabbage around the starfish.

Serves 2

Speedy Salmon Rissoles

3 large potatoes, cooked and mashed

400g canned no-added-salt pink salmon, drained and flaked

145g grated pumpkin

3 spring onions, chopped

1 tbsp German mustard

1 tbsp low-fat natural yoghurt

1 egg white

2 tsps lemon juice

125g wholemeal breadcrumbs, made from stale bread

2 tsps polyunsaturated vegetable oil

1 Place potatoes, salmon, pumpkin, spring onions, mustard, yoghurt, egg white and lemon juice in a bowl and mix to combine. Shape mixture into eight patties and roll in breadcrumbs to coat. Place patties on a plate lined with plastic food wrap and chill for 30 minutes.

2 Heat oil in a nonstick frying pan over a medium heat, add patties and cook for 3–4 minutes each side or until golden.

Serves 4

Vegetable Main Meals

Autumn Twigs and Leaves

For the 'leaves'

125g pumpkin, peeled and cut into chunks

1 small yellow capsicum, deseeded and cut into chunks

1 small red onion, quartered

4 cherry tomatoes

2 tsps olive oil, plus extra for greasing

1 tbsp balsamic vinegar

60g mixed salad leaves

For the 'twigs'

100g ready-rolled puff pastry

30g cheddar, finely grated

For the dressing

2 tbsps mayonnaise

$1/2$ tsp wholegrain mustard

1 small clove garlic, crushed

black pepper

1 Preheat the oven to 190°C. Put the pumpkin, capsicum (pepper), onion and tomatoes into a roasting tin. Sprinkle with the oil and balsamic vinegar and roast in the centre of the oven for 25 minutes or until soft and slightly browned, turning once.

2 Meanwhile, make the twigs. Lay the puff pastry on a floured surface and cut into 1cm strips. Place on a greased baking sheet and sprinkle with the cheese. Bake at the top of the oven for 10 minutes or until crisp and golden.

3 To make the dressing, mix together the mayonnaise, mustard, garlic and black pepper. To serve, arrange the salad leaves and roasted vegetables on small plates. Serve with spoonfuls of the dressing and the cheesy twigs.

Serves 2

Note: This salad of warm roasted vegetables is a real favourite when it's served with cheese sticks and a tangy dressing.

Oven temperature 190°C

Satay Vegetables

2 tsps vegetable oil
12 snow peas, trimmed and halved
375g canned baby sweetcorn, drained
60g chopped broccoli
15g bean sprouts
¼ red capsicum, chopped
60g peanut butter
1 tbsp reduced-salt soy sauce
60mL water

1 Heat oil in a frying pan over a medium heat, add snow peas, sweetcorn, broccoli, bean sprouts and red capsicum and stir-fry for 3 minutes.

2 Add peanut butter, soy sauce and water and cook, stirring, for 4 minutes longer or until vegetables are tender.

Serves 2–4

Two Foot Pie

15g butter
1 small onion, finely chopped
1 small clove garlic, crushed
1 small parsnip, finely chopped
1 small carrot, finely chopped
100g canned green lentils, drained and rinsed
200g can chopped tomatoes
1 tbsp dried mixed herbs
4 tbsps vegetable stock
black pepper, to taste

For the 'feet'
100g self-raising flour
pinch of dry mustard
15g chilled butter, cubed
30g Cheddar, grated
4 tbsps soured cream
1 small egg, beaten, to glaze

1   Heat the butter in a frying pan, then add the onion and cook for 5 minutes or until softened. Add the garlic, parsnip and carrot and cook for a further 5 minutes until softened slightly. Add the lentils, tomatoes, herbs, vegetable stock and pepper to the pan and cook gently for 25 minutes, stirring occasionally, until the vegetables are tender. Preheat the oven to 200°C.

2   Meanwhile, make the 'two foot' scones. Sift the flour and mustard into a bowl. Rub the butter into the flour mixture with your fingertips until it resembles fine breadcrumbs. Add the Cheddar and soured cream, then mix with a fork to form a dough. Knead on a floured surface until pliable. Press or roll out to a thickness of 1cm, then shape into feet.

3   Spoon the vegetable mixture into an ovenproof dish. Place the scone feet on top, then brush with beaten egg. Bake for 25 minutes or until the feet are well risen.

Serves 4

Note: Who's been walking in my pie? Children will adore this winter-warming vegetable and lentil pie, topped with its ingeniously shaped footprints.

Oven temperature 200°C

Veggie Bangers and Potatoes

1 large potato, cut into 1cm slices

1 tbsp vegetable oil

½ onion, chopped

4 vegetarian sausages, halved widthways

1 small parsnip, sliced

1 eating apple, peeled, cored and sliced

1 small carrot, sliced

1 small zucchini, sliced

1 tbsp tomato purée

200mL vegetable stock

125mL apple juice

black pepper, to taste

1 tbsp full-fat milk

1 Preheat the oven to 190°C. Boil the potato slices for 10–15 minutes, until just tender, then drain. Meanwhile, heat the oil in a heavy-based frying pan. Add the onion and sausages and fry for 5 minutes or until the onion has softened and the sausages have browned.

2 Add the parsnip, apple, carrot, zucchini, tomato purée, vegetable stock and apple juice, then stir well. Season with black pepper, then transfer to an ovenproof dish. Arrange the potato slices over the top and brush with milk. Cook, covered, for 40 minutes. Raise the heat to 220°C, then uncover and cook for another 20 minutes to brown the potato.

Serves 2

Note: Most children love sausages of any description, and both meat and vegetarian ones go really well with this fruity vegetable hotpot and its lid of crispy potatoes.

Oven temperature 190°C

Tomato Shells

2 tomatoes, halved
60g rice, cooked
2 tbsps chopped green capsicum
4 dried apricots, chopped
½ avocado, chopped
1 tbsp mayonnaise

1 Cut off tops of tomatoes and scoop out flesh, leaving shells intact. Chop tops and flesh into pieces and place in a bowl.

2 Add rice, green capsicum, apricots, avocado and mayonnaise and toss to combine. Spoon filling into shells.

Makes 2

Fruit and Cheese Waldolf

1–2 seedless oranges, segmented
90g chopped or shredded red
or green cabbage
1 red or green apple, diced
2 stalks celery, diagonally sliced
2 tbsps sultanas
2 tbsps chopped pitted prunes or dates
2 tbsps diced dried apricots

Cheese and nut dressing
185g cottage or ricotta cheese
90mL milk or
60g natural yoghurt
30g pinenuts or unsalted peanuts,
finely chopped

1 Cut orange segments in half and place in a bowl. Add cabbage, apple, celery, sultanas, prunes or dates and apricots and toss to combine.

2 To make dressing, place cottage or ricotta cheese and milk or yoghurt in a bowl and whisk until creamy. Add nuts and mix to combine. Spoon dressing over salad and serve.

Serves 4

Vegetables with Cheesy Potatoes

60mL olive oil

1 onion, chopped

1 eggplant, cubed

1 green or red capsicum, chopped

2 zucchini, halved lengthwise and sliced

400g canned tomatoes, undrained and roughly chopped

90g green beans, halved or sliced

90g butter or yellow wax beans, halved or sliced

170mL vegetable stock

1 tbsp tomato paste (purée)

Cheesy Potato Topping

500g potatoes, chopped

3–4 tbsps milk

60g grated tasty cheese (mature cheddar)

1 Heat oil in a large saucepan over a medium heat, add onion and cook, stirring, for 3–4 minutes or until onion is soft. Add eggplant, cover and cook for 5 minutes.

2 Add green or red capsicum, zucchini and tomatoes to pan and cook, stirring occasionally, for 5 minutes. Add green beans, butter or yellow wax beans, stock and tomato paste and bring to simmering. Simmer, uncovered, for 15 minutes or until vegetables are tender and mixture reduces and thickens.

3 To make topping, boil, steam or microwave potatoes until tender. Place in a bowl with milk and mash.

4 Transfer vegetable mixture to an oiled baking or casserole dish or casserole. Top with potatoes, sprinkle with cheese and bake for 15 minutes or until topping is golden.

Serves 4

Egg Foo Yung with Peas

60g snow peas, trimmed
60g sugar snap peas, trimmed
3 eggs
60mL water
1½ tsp reduced-salt soy sauce
1 tsp sesame oil
1 tbsp vegetable oil
30g bean sprouts
1 spring onion, finely chopped

1 Boil, steam or microwave snow peas and sugar snap peas until just tender. Drain. Refresh under cold running water, drain again and pat dry with absorbent kitchen paper.

2 Place eggs, water, soy sauce and sesame oil in a bowl and whisk lightly to combine. Heat vegetable oil in a frying pan over a medium heat, add egg mixture and stir-fry for 1 minute, or until egg just begins to set. Add snow peas, sugar snap peas, bean sprouts and spring onion and stir-fry for 1 minute longer. Cool slightly and serve.

Serves 2

Bean Frittata

1 tsp vegetable oil
½ tomato, chopped
90g canned three bean mix
2 eggs, lightly beaten
60mL milk
30g grated tasty cheese
(mature cheddar)

1 Heat oil in a small frying pan over a medium heat, add tomato and cook for 1 minute or until soft. Add beans and mix to combine.

2 Place eggs, milk and cheese in a bowl and whisk to combine. Pour egg mixture over bean mixture in pan and cook over a low heat, without stirring, for 5 minutes or until frittata is firm.

Serves 2

Gado Gado

2 potatoes
200g green beans
¹/4 savoy cabbage
2 carrots
1 cucumber
hard boiled eggs
lettuce leaves
bottled satay or peanut sauce

1 Slice and cook potatoes, top and tail beans and cook until bright green. Cool potatoes and beans. Thinly slice and wash the cabbage, grate the carrots and slice the cucumber.

2 Place the lettuce on a large platter, arrange the vegetables and eggs over the lettuce. Spoon the satay or peanut sauce over the vegetables.

Serves 4

Vegetable Risotto

1 tbsp vegetable oil
1 small onion, chopped
125g carrots, finely diced or grated
60g button mushrooms, sliced
170g short-grain rice
90g zucchini, sliced
1/4 red or green capsicums, sliced
30g frozen peas
250mL tomato or vegetable juice
125mL vegetable or chicken stock
45g grated tasty cheese
(mature cheddar)
toasted pinenuts or sesame seeds

1   Heat oil in a saucepan over a medium heat, add onion, carrots and mushrooms and cook, stirring, for 3–4 minutes or until onion is soft. Add rice, zucchini and red or green capsicum or peas and cook, stirring, for 2 minutes longer.

2   Stir tomato or vegetable juice and stock into mixture and bring to the boil. Reduce heat, cover and simmer for 12–15 minutes or until rice is tender and liquid is absorbed. Sprinkle with cheese and pinenuts or sesame seeds and serve.

Serves 4

Creamy Vegetable Pasta

125g pasta of your choice
2 tsps vegetable oil
125g chopped cauliflower
125g chopped broccoli
1 zucchini, chopped
1 carrot, chopped or grated
125g cream cheese, softened
3 tbsps milk

1 Cook pasta in boiling water in a saucepan following packet directions. Drain, set aside and keep warm.

2 Heat oil in a frying pan over a medium heat, add cauliflower, broccoli, zucchini and carrot and cook, stirring, for 3–4 minutes or until vegetables are just tender.

3 Stir cream cheese and milk into pan and, stirring, bring to simmering. Simmer for 4 minutes. Spoon vegetable mixture over pasta and serve.

Serves 2

Mushroom Penne

125g penne pasta

Mushroom sauce
1 tbsp olive oil
125g button mushrooms, sliced
2 tbsps vegetable stock
2 tbsps sour cream
2 tsps chopped fresh parsley

1 Cook pasta in boiling water in a saucepan following packet directions. Drain, set aside and keep warm.

2 To make sauce, heat oil in a frying pan over a medium heat, add mushrooms and cook, stirring, for 4 minutes. Add stock and sour cream to pan and cook for 2 minutes longer. Stir in parsley and spoon sauce over pasta. Toss to combine and serve.

Serves 1

Puddings and Cakes

Lamingtons Photographed page 70

1 pre-baked butter or sponge cake,
18 x 28cm
500g icing sugar
3 tbsps cocoa powder
6–8 tbsps warm water
500g desiccated coconut

1   Cut sponge into twelve squares. Set aside.
2   Place icing sugar and cocoa powder in sifter or sieve.
Sift into large bowl.
3   Stir in water until you have a runny icing. Pour icing into one
of the shallow cake tins. Place coconut in the other tin.
4   Using tongs or two forks dip cake squares in chocolate icing.
Remove cake from icing. Allow excess icing to drain off. Roll
in coconut. Place Lamingtons on wire rack to set.

Makes 12

Hop Scotch

100g butterscotch sweets
500g tub vanilla ice cream
312g can mandarins, drained
3 Cadbury chocolate flakes

1   Put the butterscotch sweets into a strong plastic bag. Roughly
crush with a rolling pin.
2   Place the ice cream in a large bowl and mash with a fork.
Mix in the crushed butterscotch. Return to the container and
freeze for 1–2 hours.
3   Transfer the ice cream to the fridge for 20 minutes before
serving to soften slightly. Place the mandarins in sundae
glasses, together with 2 scoops of ice cream. Crush one of
the chocolate flakes and sprinkle over the top of the ice cream.
Cut the remaining flakes in half and push 1 into each serving.

Serves 4

Note: Hop, skip and crunch! This is the sort of pudding that children
dream of. It's really quick to make, which is just as well – you'll probably
be asked for it again and again.

Apple Roll-ups

60g plain flour
150mL full-fat milk
1 medium egg
finely grated rind of ½ small orange
30g butter, melted, plus extra for frying
maple syrup to serve

For the filling
2 eating apples, peeled, cored and chopped
½ tsp ground cinnamon
1 tbsp water

1 To make the batter, blend the flour, milk, egg, orange rind and melted butter until smooth in a food processor or using a hand blender. Leave it to rest for 20 minutes.

2 Meanwhile, make the filling. Put the apples, cinnamon and 1 tablespoon of water into a small saucepan, cover, and cook gently for 5–7 minutes, stirring occasionally, until the apples have softened.

3 Melt just enough butter to cover the base of a 18cm non-stick frying pan. Pour in a quarter of the batter and tilt the pan so that it covers the base. Cook for 1–2 minutes on each side, until golden. Keep warm and repeat to make 3 more pancakes, greasing the pan when necessary.

4 Place 2 pancakes on each plate. Fill with the apple mixture and carefully roll up. Serve with maple syrup.

Serves 2

Note: Roll up, roll up…for these hot apple-filled pancakes, served with maple syrup. Try them with a generous dollop of creamy yogurt or a scoop of vanilla ice cream.

Rocky Road Ice Cream

2 x 60g chocolate-coated Turkish delight bars

20 marshmallows

12 glacé cherries

2 x 45g chocolate nut bars

1 litre softened chocolate ice cream

30g desiccated coconut

1 Chop Turkish delight bars. Set aside.

2 Chop marshmallows. Set aside.

3 Chop cherries. Set aside.

4 Chop chocolate nut bars. Set aside.

5 Place ice cream in bowl. Add Turkish delight bars, marshmallows, cherries, nut bars and coconut. Mix.

6 Spoon into freezerproof container. Cover with plastic food wrap. Freeze.

Serves 6

Muddy Puddles

75g chocolate digestive biscuits
75g butter
75g plain milk chocolate
2 tbsps golden syrup
1 medium egg, beaten
few drops of vanilla essence
15g white chocolate

1 Put the biscuits into a plastic bag, seal, then crush with a rolling pin. Melt 30g of the butter in a saucepan. Remove from the heat and mix in the biscuits. Line a muffin tin with 4 paper muffin cases. Divide the biscuit mixture between them, pressing over the base and sides of each case with the back of a teaspoon. Refrigerate for 20 minutes or until firm.

2 Preheat the oven to 180°C. Meanwhile, put the remaining butter, plain chocolate and syrup into a bowl set over a saucepan of simmering water. Heat gently, stirring, until melted. Remove from the heat and cool for 5 minutes. Whisk in the egg and vanilla essence.

3 Spoon the chocolate mixture over the biscuit bases and bake for 20 minutes or until just firm. Leave to cool for 10 minutes. Meanwhile, melt the white chocolate in a bowl set over a pan of simmering water, then drizzle over the puddles.

Makes 4

Note: *Chocoholic children (or adults) will adore these pools of chocolate. They've got a chocolate biscuit base, a creamy chocolate filling and even more drizzled on top. Heaven!*

Oven temperature 180°C

Glossary

Acidulated water: water with added acid, such as lemon juice or vinegar, which prevents discolouration of ingredients, particularly fruit or vegetables. The proportion of acid to water is 1 teaspoon per 300mL.

Al dente: Italian cooking term for ingredients that are cooked until tender but still firm to the bite; usually applied to pasta.

Américaine: method of serving seafood, usually lobster and monkfish, in a sauce flavoured with olive oil, aromatic herbs, tomatoes, white wine, fish stock, brandy and tarragon.

Anglaise: cooking style for simple cooked dishes such as boiled vegetables. Assiette anglaise is a plate of cold cooked meats.

Antipasto: Italian for 'before the meal', it denotes an assortment of cold meats, vegetables and cheeses, often marinated, served as an hors d'oeuvre. A typical antipasto might include salami, prosciutto, marinated artichoke hearts, anchovy fillets, olives, tuna fish and provolone cheese.

Au gratin: food sprinkled with breadcrumbs, often covered with cheese sauce and browned until a crisp coating forms.

Bain marie: a saucepan standing in a large pan which is filled with boiling water to keep liquids at simmering point. A double boiler will do the same job.

Balsamic vinegar: a mild, extremely fragrant, wine-based vinegar made in northern Italy. Traditionally, the vinegar is aged for at least seven years in a series of casks made of various woods.

Baste: to moisten food while it is cooking by spooning or brushing on liquid or fat.

Beat: to stir thoroughly and vigorously.

Beurre manie: equal quantities of butter and flour kneaded together and added, a little at a time, to thicken a stew or casserole.

bird: see *paupiette*.

Blanc: a cooking liquid made by adding flour and lemon juice to water in order to keep certain vegetables from discolouring as they cook.

Blanch: to plunge into boiling water and then, in some cases, into cold water. Fruits and nuts are blanched to remove skin easily.

Blanquette: a white stew of lamb, veal or chicken, bound with egg yolks and cream and accompanied by onion and mushrooms.

blend: to mix thoroughly.

Bonne femme: dishes cooked in the traditional French 'housewife' style. Chicken and pork *bonne femme* are garnished with bacon, potatoes and baby onion; fish *bonne femme* with mushrooms in a white-wine sauce.

Bouquet garni: a bunch of herbs, usually consisting of sprigs of parsley, thyme, marjoram, rosemary, a bay leaf, peppercorns and cloves, tied in muslin and used to flavour stews and casseroles.

Braise: to cook whole or large pieces of poultry, game, fish, meat or vegetables in a small amount of wine, stock or other liquid in a closed pot. Often the main ingredient is first browned in fat and then cooked in a low oven or very slowly on top of the stove. Braising suits tough meats and older birds and produces a mellow, rich sauce.

Broil: the American term for grilling food.

Brown: cook in a small amount of fat until brown.

Burghul (also bulgur): a type of cracked wheat, where the kernels are steamed and dried before being crushed.

Buttered: to spread with softened or melted butter.

Butterfly: to slit a piece of food in half horizontally, cutting it almost through so that when opened it resembles butterfly wings. Chops, large prawns and thick fish fillets are often butterflied so that they cook more quickly.

Buttermilk: a tangy, low-fat cultured milk product; its slight acidity makes it an ideal marinade base for poultry.

Calzone: a semicircular pocket of pizza dough, stuffed with meat or vegetables, sealed and baked.

Caramelise: to melt sugar until it is a golden-brown syrup.

Champignons: small mushrooms, usually canned.

Chasseur: French for 'hunter'; a French cooking style in which meat and chicken dishes are cooked with mushrooms, spring onions, white wine and often tomato.

Clarify: to melt butter and drain the oil off the sediment.

Coat: to cover with a thin layer of flour, sugar, nuts, crumbs, poppy or sesame seeds, cinnamon sugar or a few of the ground spices.

Concasser: to chop coarsely, usually tomatoes.

Confit: from the French verb *confire*, meaning to preserve, food that is made into a preserve by cooking very slowly and thoroughly until tender. In the case of meat, such as duck or goose, it is cooked in its own fat, and covered with the fat so that the meat does not come into contact with the air. Vegetables such as onions are good in confit.

Consommé: a clear soup usually made from beef.

Coulis: a thin purée, usually of fresh or cooked fruit or vegetables, which is soft enough to pour (in French *couler* means 'to run'). A coulis may be rough-textured or very smooth.

Court bouillon: the liquid in which fish, poultry or meat is cooked. It usually consists of water with bay leaf, onion, carrots and salt and freshly ground black pepper to taste. Other additives may include wine, vinegar, stock, garlic or spring (green) onions.

Couscous: cereal processed from semolina into pellets, traditionally steamed and served with meat and vegetables in the classic North African stew of the same name.

Cream: to make soft, smooth and creamy by rubbing with the back of a spoon or by beating with a mixer. Usually applied to fat and sugar.

Croutons: small toasted or fried cubes of bread.

Cruciferous vegetables: certain members of the mustard, cabbage and turnip families with cross-shaped flowers and strong aromas and flavours.

Crudités: raw vegetables, cut in slices or sticks to nibble plain or with a dipping sauce, or shredded vegetables tossed as salad with a simple dressing.

Cube: to cut into small pieces with six equal sides.

Curdle: to cause milk or sauce to separate into solid and liquid. Example, overcooked egg mixtures.

Daikon radish (also called mooli): a long white Japanese radish.

Dark sesame oil (also called Oriental sesame oil): dark polyunsaturated oil with a low burning point, used for seasoning. Do not replace with lighter sesame oil.

Deglaze: to dissolve congealed cooking juices or glaze on the bottom of a pan by adding a liquid, then scraping and stirring vigorously whilst bringing the liquid to the boil. Juices may be used to make gravy or to add to sauce.

Degrease: to skim grease from the surface of liquid. If possible the liquid should be chilled so the fat solidifies. If not, skim off most of the fat with a large metal spoon, then trail strips of paper towel on the surface of the liquid to remove any remaining globules.

Devilled: a dish or sauce that is highly seasoned with a hot ingredient such as mustard, Worcestershire sauce or cayenne pepper.

Dice: to cut into small cubes.

Dietary fibre: a plant-cell material that is undigested or only partially digested in the human body, but which promotes healthy digestion of other food matter.

Dissolve: mix a dry ingredient with liquid until absorbed.

Dredge: to coat with a dry ingredient, such as flour or sugar.

Drizzle: to pour in a fine thread-like stream over a surface.

Dust: to sprinkle or coat lightly with flour or icing sugar.

Dutch oven: a heavy casserole with a lid usually made from cast iron or pottery.

Emulsion: a mixture of two liquids that are not mutually soluble; for example, oil and water.

Entrée: in Europe, the 'entry' or hors d'oeuvre; in North America entree means the main course.

Fenugreek: a small, slender annual herb of the pea family. The seeds are spice. Ground fenugreek has a strong maple sweetness, spicy but bitter flavour and an aroma of burnt sugar.

Fillet: special cut of beef, lamb, pork or veal; breast of poultry and game; fish cut off the bone lengthwise.

Flake: to break into small pieces with a fork.

Flame: to ignite warmed alcohol over food.

Fold in: a gentle, careful combining of a light or delicate mixture with a heavier mixture, using a metal spoon.

Frenched: when fat and gristle is scraped and cut from meat on a bone, leaving the meaty part virtually fat free.

Fricassé: a dish in which poultry, fish or vegetables are bound together with a white or velouté sauce. In Britain and the United States, the name applies to an old-fashioned dish of chicken in a creamy sauce.

Galangal: A member of the ginger family, commonly known as Laos or Siamese ginger. It has a peppery taste with overtones of ginger.

Galette: sweet or savoury mixture shaped as a flat round.

Ganache: a filling or glaze made of full cream, chocolate, and/or other flavourings, often used to sandwich the layers of gourmet chocolate cakes

Garnish: to decorate food, usually with something edible.

Gastrique: caramelised sugar deglazed with vinegar and used in fruit-flavoured savoury sauces, in such dishes as duck with orange.

Ghee: butter, clarified by boiling. Commonly used in Indian cooking.

Glaze: a thin coating of beaten egg, syrup or aspic which is brushed over pastry, fruits or cooked meats.

Gluten: a protein in flour that is developed when dough is kneaded, making the dough elastic.

Gratin: a dish cooked in the oven or under the grill so that it develops a brown crust. Breadcrumbs or cheese may be sprinkled on top first. Shallow gratin dishes ensure a maximum area of crust.

Grease: to rub or brush lightly with oil or fat.

Infuse: to immerse herbs, spices or other flavourings in hot liquid to flavour it. Infusion takes 2–5 minutes depending on the flavouring. The liquid should be very hot but not boiling.

Jardinière: a garnish of garden vegetables, typically carrots, pickling onions, French beans and turnips.

Joint: to cut poultry, game or small animals into serving pieces by dividing at the joint.

Julienne: to cut food into match-like strips.

Lights: lungs of an animal, used in various meat preparations such as pates and faggots.

Line: to cover the inside of a container with paper, to protect or aid in removing mixture.

Knead: to work dough using heel of hand with a pressing motion, while stretching and folding the dough.

Macerate: to soak food in liquid to soften.

Marinade: a seasoned liquid, usually an oil and acid mixture, in which meats or other foods are soaked to soften and give more flavour.

Marinara: Italian 'sailor's style' cooking that does not apply to any particular combination of ingredients. Marinara tomato sauce for pasta is the most familiar.

Marinate: to let food stand in a marinade to season and tenderise.

Mask: to cover cooked food with sauce.

Melt: to heat until liquified.

Mince: to grind into very small pieces.

Mix: to combine ingredients by stirring.

Monounsaturated fats: one of three types of fats found in foods. It is believed these fats do not raise the level of cholesterol in the blood.

Naan: a slightly leavened bread used in Indian cooking.

Niçoise: a garnish of tomatoes, garlic and black olives; a salad with anchovy, tuna and French beans is typical.

Noisette: small 'nut' of lamb cut from boned loin or rack that is rolled, tied and cut in neat slices. Noisette also means flavoured with hazelnuts, or butter cooked to a nut brown colour.

Non-reactive pan: a cooking pan whose surface does not chemically react with food. Materials used include stainless steel, enamel, glass and some alloys.

Normande: a cooking style for fish, with a garnish of prawn, mussels and mushrooms in a white-wine cream sauce; for poultry and meat, a sauce with cream, calvados and apple.

Olive oil: various grades of oil extracted from olives. Extra virgin olive oil has a full, fruity flavour and the lowest acidity. Virgin olive oil is slightly higher in acidity and lighter in flavour. Pure olive oil is a processed blend of olive oils and has the highest acidity and lightest taste.

Panade: a mixture for binding stuffings and dumplings, notably quenelles (fish rissoles), often of choux pastry or simply breadcrumbs. A panade may also be made of frangipane, puréed potatoes or rice.

Papillote: to cook in oiled or buttered greasepoof paper or aluminum foil. Also a decorative frill to cover bone ends of chops and poultry drumsticks.

Parboil: to boil or simmer until part cooked (i.e. cooked further than when blanching).

Pare: to cut away outside covering.

Pâté: a paste of meat or seafood used as a spread for toast or crackers.

Paupiette: a thin slice of meat, poultry or fish spread with a savoury stuffing and rolled. In the United States this is also called 'bird' and in Britain an 'olive'.

Peel: to strip away outside covering.

Plump: to soak in liquid or moisten thoroughly until full and round.

Poach: to simmer gently in enough hot liquid to cover, using care to retain shape of food.

Polyunsaturated fat: one of the three types of fats found in food. These exist in large quantities in such vegetable oils as safflower, sunflower, corn and soya bean. These fats lower the level of cholesterol in the blood.

Purée: a smooth paste, usually of vegetables or fruits, made by putting foods through a sieve, food mill or liquefying in a blender or food processor.

Ragout: traditionally a well-seasoned, rich stew containing meat, vegetables and wine. Nowadays, a term applied to any stewed mixture.

Ramekins: small oval or round individual baking dishes.

Reconstitute: to put moisture back into dehydrated foods by soaking in liquid.

Reduce: to cook over a very high heat, uncovered, until the liquid is reduced by evaporation.

Refresh: to cool hot food quickly, either under running water or by plunging it into iced water, to stop it cooking. Particularly for vegetables and occasionally for shellfish.

Rice vinegar: mild, fragrant vinegar that is less sweet than cider vinegar and not as harsh as distilled malt vinegar. Japanese rice vinegar is milder than the Chinese variety.

Roulade: a piece of meat, usually pork or veal, that is spread with stuffing, rolled and often braised or poached. A roulade may also be a sweet or savoury mixture that is baked in a Swiss-roll tin or paper case, filled with a contrasting filling, and rolled.

Roux: A binding for sauces, made with flour and butter or another fatty substance, to which a hot liquid is added. A roux-based sauce may be white, blond or brown, depending on how the butter has been cooked.

Rubbing-in: a method of incorporating fat into flour, by use of fingertips only. Also incorporates air into mixture.

Safflower oil: the vegetable oil that contains the highest proportion of polyunsaturated fats.

Salsa: a juice derived from the main ingredient being cooked, or a sauce added to a dish to enhance its flavour. In Italy the term is often used for pasta sauces; in Mexico the name usually applies to uncooked sauces served as an accompaniment, especially to corn chips.

Saturated fats: one of the three types of fats found in foods. These exist in large quantities in animal products, coconut and palm oils; they raise the level of cholesterol in the blood. As high cholesterol levels may cause heart disease, saturated-fat consumption is recommended to be less than 15 percent of calories provided by the daily diet.

Sauté: to cook or brown in small amount of hot fat.

Scald: to bring just to boiling point, usually for milk. Also to rinse with boiling water.

School prawns: delicious eaten just on their own. Smaller prawn than bay, tiger or king. They have a mild flavour, low oiliness and high moisture content, they make excellent cocktails.

Score: to mark food with cuts, notches or lines to prevent curling or to make food more attractive.

Sear: to brown surface quickly over high heat in hot dish.

Seasoned flour: flour with salt and pepper added.

Sift: to shake a dry, powdered substance through a sieve or sifter to remove any lumps and give lightness.

Simmer: to cook food gently in liquid that bubbles steadily just below boiling point so that the food cooks in even heat without breaking up.

Singe: to quickly flame poultry to remove all traces of feathers after plucking.

Skim: to remove a surface layer (often of impurities and scum) from a liquid with a metal spoon or small ladle.

Slivered: sliced in long, thin pieces, usually refers to nuts, especially almonds.

Souse: to cover food, particularly fish, in wine vinegar and spices and cook slowly; the food is cooled in the same liquid. Sousing gives food a pickled flavour.

Steep: to soak in warm or cold liquid in order to soften food and draw out strong flavours or impurities.

Stir-fry: to cook thin slices of meat and vegetable over a high heat in a small amount of oil, stirring constantly to even cooking in a short time. Traditionally cooked in a wok; however, a heavy-based frying pan may be used.

Stock: the liquid that results from cooking meat, bones and/or vegetables in water to make a base for soups and other recipes. You can substitute stock cubes for fresh bouillon, but those on a reduced sodium diet will need to take note of the salt content on the packet.

Stud: to adorn with; for example, baked ham studded with whole cloves.

Sugo: an Italian sauce made from the liquid or juice extracted from fruit or meat during cooking.

Sweat: to cook sliced or chopped food, usually vegetables, in a little fat and no liquid over very low heat. Foil is pressed on top so that the food steams in its own juices, usually before being added to other dishes.

Thicken: to make a liquid thicker by mixing together arrowroot, cornflour or flour with an equal amount of cold water and pouring it into hot liquid, cooking and stirring until thickened.

Timbale: a creamy mixture of vegetables or meat baked in a mould. French for 'kettledrum'; also denotes a drum-shaped baking dish.

Toss: to gently mix ingredients with two forks or fork and spoon.

Total fat: the individual daily intake of all three fats previously described in this glossary. Nutritionists recommend that fats provide no more than 35 percent of the energy in the diet.

Vine leaves: tender, lightly flavoured leaves of the grapevine, used in ethnic cuisine as wrappers for savoury mixtures. As the leaves are usually packed in brine, they should be well rinsed before use.

Whip: to beat rapidly, incorporate air and produce expansion.

Zest: thin outer layer of citrus fruits containing the aromatic citrus oil. It is usually thinly pared with a vegetable peeler, or grated with a zester or grater to separate it from the bitter white pith underneath.

Weights and Measures

Cooking is not an exact science. You do not require finely calibrated scales, pipettes and scientific equipment to cook, yet the variety of measures in countries have confused many a good cook.

Although different in the recipes weights are given for ingredients such as meats, fish, poultry and some vegetables, in normal cooking a few ounces or grams one way or another will not affect the success of your dish.

Although recipes have been tested using the Australian Standard 250mL cup, 20mL tablespoon (tbsp) and 5mL teaspoon (tsp), they will work just as well with the US and Canadian 8fl oz cup, or the UK 300mL cup. We have used graduated cup measures in preference to tablespoon measures so that proportions are always the same. Where tablespoon measures have been given, they are not crucial measures, so using the smaller tablespoon of the US or UK will not affect the recipe's success. At least all three countries agree on the teaspoon size.

For breads, cakes and pastries, the only area which might cause concern is where eggs are used, as proportions will then vary. If working with a 250mL or 300mL cup, use large eggs (65g/$2\frac{1}{4}$oz), adding a little more liquid to the recipe for 300mL cup measures if it seems necessary. Use medium-sized eggs (55g/2oz) with an 8fl oz cup measure. A graduated set of measuring cups and spoons is recommended for measuring dry ingredients. Remember to level the ingredients in the measure to ensure an accurate quantity.

English Measures

English measurements are all similar to Australian with two exceptions: the English cup measures 300mL/$10\frac{1}{2}$ fl oz, whereas the American and Australian cup measures 250mL/$8\frac{3}{4}$fl oz. The English tablespoon (the Australian dessertspoon) measures 14.8mL /$\frac{1}{2}$ fl oz against Australian tablespoon of 20mL/$\frac{3}{4}$fl oz. The Imperial measurement is 20fl oz to the pint, 40fl oz a quart and 160fl oz one gallon.

American Measures

The American reputed pint is 16fl oz, a quart is equal to 32fl oz and the American gallon equals 128fl oz. The American tablespoon is equal to 14.8mL/$\frac{1}{2}$ fl oz, while the teaspoon is 5mL/$\frac{1}{6}$ fl oz. The cup measure is 250 mL/$8\frac{3}{4}$ fl oz.

Dry Measures

All the measures are level, so when you have filled a cup or spoon, level it off with the edge of a knife. The scale below is the 'cook's equivalent'; it is not an exact conversion of metric to imperial measurement. To calculate the exact metric equivalent yourself, multiply ounces by 28.349523 to obtain grams, or divide grams by 28.349523 to obtain ounces.

Metric grams (g), kilograms (kg)	Imperial ounces (oz), pound (lb)
15g	$\frac{1}{2}$oz
20g	$\frac{1}{3}$oz
30g	1oz
55g	2oz
85g	3oz
115g	4oz/$\frac{1}{4}$lb
125g	$4\frac{1}{2}$oz
140/145g	5oz
170g	6oz
200g	7oz
225g	8oz/$\frac{1}{2}$lb
315g	11oz
340g	12oz/$\frac{3}{4}$lb
370g	13oz
400g	14oz
425g	15oz
455g	16oz/1lb
1,000g/1 kg	35.3oz/2.2lb
1.5kg	3.33lb

Oven Temperatures

The Celsius temperatures given here are not exact; they have been rounded off and are given as a guide only. Follow the manufacturer's oven guide, relating it to the temperature description given in the recipe. Remember gas ovens are hottest at the top, electric ovens at the bottom and convection-fan forced ovens are usually even throughout. We have included Regulo numbers for gas cookers which may assist. To convert °C to °F multiply °C by 9 and divide by 5 then add 32.

	C°	F°	Gas mark
Very slow	120	250	1
Slow	150	300	2
Moderately slow	160	325	3
Moderate	180	350	4
Moderately hot	190–200	370–400	5–6
Hot	210–220	410–440	6–7
Very hot	230	450	8
Super hot	250–290	475–500	9–10

Cup Measurements

One Australian cup (250mL) is equal to the following weights.

	Metric	Imperial
Almonds, flaked	85g	3oz
Almonds, kernel	155g	5$\frac{1}{2}$oz
Almonds, slivered, ground	125g	4$\frac{1}{2}$oz
Apples, dried, chopped	125g	4$\frac{1}{2}$oz
Apricots, dried, chopped	190g	6$\frac{3}{4}$oz
Breadcrumbs, packet	125g	4$\frac{1}{2}$oz
Breadcrumbs, soft	55g	2oz
Cheese, grated	115g	4oz
Chocbits	155$\frac{1}{2}$g	5oz
Coconut, desiccated	90g	3oz
Cornflakes	30g	1oz
Currants	155$\frac{1}{2}$g	5oz
Flour	115g	4oz
Fruit, dried (mixed, sultanas etc)	170g	6 oz
Ginger, crystallised, glace	250g	8oz
Honey, treacle, golden syrup	315g	11oz
Mixed peel	225g	8oz
Nuts, chopped	115g	4oz
Prunes, chopped	225g	8oz
Rice, cooked	155g	5$\frac{1}{2}$oz
Rice, uncooked	225g	8oz
Rolled oats	90g	3oz
Sesame seeds	115g	4oz
Shortening (butter, margarine)	225g	8oz
Sugar, brown	155g	5$\frac{1}{2}$oz
Sugar, granulated or caster	225g	8oz
Sugar, sifted icing	155g	5$\frac{1}{2}$oz
Wheatgerm	60g	2oz

Length

Some of us have trouble converting imperial length to metric. In this scale, measures have been rounded off to the easiest figures. To convert inches to centimetres exactly, multiply inches by 2.54. One inch equals 25.4 millimetres and 1 millimetre equals 0.03937 inches.

Cake Dish Sizes

Metric	15cm	18cm	20cm	23cm
Imperial	6in	7in	8in	9in

Loaf Dish Sizes

Metric	23 x 12cm	25 x 8cm	28 x 18cm
Imperial	9 x 5in	10 x 3in	11 x 7in

Liquid Measures

Metric millilitres (mL)	Imperial fluid ounce (fl oz)	Cup and Spoon
5mL	$\frac{1}{6}$fl oz	1 teaspoon
20mL	$\frac{2}{3}$fl oz	1 tablespoon
30mL	1fl oz	1 tbsp + 2 tsp
55mL	2fl oz	
63mL	2$\frac{1}{4}$fl oz	$\frac{1}{4}$ cup
85mL	3fl oz	
115mL	4fl oz	
125mL	4$\frac{1}{2}$fl oz	$\frac{1}{2}$ cup
150mL	5$\frac{1}{4}$fl oz	
188mL	6$\frac{2}{3}$fl oz	$\frac{3}{4}$ cup
225mL	8fl oz	
250mL	8$\frac{3}{4}$fl oz	1 cup
300mL	10$\frac{1}{2}$fl oz	
370mL	13fl oz	
400mL	14fl oz	
438mL	15$\frac{1}{2}$fl oz	1$\frac{3}{4}$ cups
455mL	16fl oz	
500mL	17$\frac{1}{2}$fl oz	2 cups
570mL	20fl oz	
1 litre	35.3fl oz	4 cups

Length Measures

Metric millimetres (mm), centimetres (cm)	Imperial inches (in), feet (ft)
5mm, 0.5cm	$\frac{1}{4}$in
10mm, 1.0cm	$\frac{1}{2}$in
20mm, 2.0cm	$\frac{3}{4}$in
2.5cm	1in
5cm	2in
7$\frac{1}{2}$cm	3in
10cm	4in
12$\frac{1}{2}$cm	5in
15cm	6in
18cm	7in
20cm	8in
23cm	9in
25cm	10in
28cm	11in
30cm	12in, 1 foot

Index